MOVEMENTS IN MODERN ART

EXPRESSIONISM

MOVEMENTS IN MODERN ART

EDITH HOFFMANN

EXPRESSIONISM

WITH 24 ILLUSTRATIONS

CHOSEN BY HEINRICH NEUMAYER

CROWN PUBLISHERS, INC.

NEW YORK

Reproduction Rights: S.P.A.D.E.M., Paris, and Cosmopress, Geneva
Printed in Austria
by Brüder Rosenbaum, Vienna

EXPRESSIONISM

"Expressionism" is a term which indicates precisely what it stands for. It was invented to point to a contrast: the difference between an art which was based on purely visual impressions — accordingly known as "Impressionism" — and a new movement which aimed at the expression of ideas and emotions, still, it is true, by the representation of things seen, but with emphasis on their symbolic or emotive character. Invented by art critics who were the contemporaries of the Expressionist artists, that is to say in the first decade of this century, the word "Expressionism" thus contains a whole programme. It marks a new attitude and a new method. Dissatisfied with an art that merely rendered the appearance of objects or offered a mirror of actual events, the artists of the new century wanted to penetrate deeper, to show things as they knew they were under the surface, or as they might have been had the visible and tangible world always corresponded with the intangible and spiritual. They wanted to extend the domain of art beyond the boundaries of the actual, so as to include the imagined, the dreamt and the foreseen. They wanted, more than anything else, to "express" themselves.

This longing for a revival of emotional and spiritual values in the arts, which was felt by so many writers and painters around the turn of the century, was a reaction against the materialistic attitude of the preceding generation. During the 19th century, the scientific exploration of the material world had made such progress, and this progress had been received so enthusiastically by humanity, that an objective, realistic approach in all matters, including the arts, had gradually taken the place of earlier, more romantic tendencies. Even a movement as revolutionary and as purely artistic as Impressionism was an outcome of this attitude, for the attempts of the Impressionists to draw conclusions for their art from their knowledge of the laws of optics were quite in accordance with the respect for science which all their contemporaries shared. But the decades which followed upon their experiments and first successes brought the inevitable swing of the pendulum: by 1890 the avant-garde was "symbolist", and Gauguin warned younger painters not to follow nature too closely. He told them to search their own selves rather than to look too much at their surroundings, and although he considered an art in which the human element was lacking as sterile, he disapproved of the use of models.

It was, in fact, Gauguin who put man, as it were, back into the centre of art. The Expressionists, whose leaders were mostly beginners when the French master died, went one step further: to them, too, man was the main subject of painting, but it was the artist himself who mattered more than anybody else. *His* experience, *his* emotions had to be translated into works of art. He rendered things, not objectively, but as *he* saw them. Instead of reproducing them, he recreated them according to his own mood. The artist's personality and imagination thus mattered more in the creation of Expressionist pictures than the subject he chose to paint.

The result of this new attitude was a highly subjective art. Once the laws of realism had been discarded, the artist acquired a new, almost unlimited freedom. If his pictures were no longer to be a mirror of the actual world, he could ignore the rules of perspective which painters had once struggled to establish in order to make their works look more "real". The proportions of figures and objects could be changed, details taken apart and combined in a new fashion. Familiar shapes lent themselves to distortion, and distortion could be made to serve that internal truth which was now valued more than visual harmony. Beauty was often replaced by intensity. Grotesque and even repulsive elements were admitted in order to induce a shock in the beholder. For to shock by artistic means was now permitted, and such tactics were not only favoured by artists whose works were intended to convey socialist, pacifist or other political ideas, but also by those who simply wished to shake their public out of its general lethargy.

Colour, too, was made to serve the same purpose. No longer bound to follow the impressions received by the eye, it obtained a new vigour, became more powerful and sometimes more brutal than ever before. The effect of ecstasy or obsession produced by certain Expressionist works is mainly due to the uninhibited application of strong, unmixed colours. But in some cases colour acquired yet another function: instead of reflecting the aspects of reality, it became symbolic. The period of green faces and blue horses had set in.

Popular as well as literary traditions have always insisted that certain colours correspond with certain states of mind: blue is often supposed to stand for love, red for passion, yellow for jealousy and white for innocence. The Expressionists were, of course, familiar with these ancient associations which occur in many folk songs as well as in the writings of Goethe and the Romantics, and they were naturally pre-occupied with the nature and effect of colour. Equally interested in psychology, as some of them were — it is worth remembering that theirs was the age of Freud's first triumphs, and "the inner eye" was a formula much used by artists and art critics alike — they certainly made at least half-conscious use of the suggestive qualities of colour. It became a dynamic element which contributed to the dramatic character of their work. For Expressionism was rarely a lyrical, and very often a dramatic style, and it is because of this that it has been called a romantic movement.

The dramatisation so typical of many Expressionist works was frequently a self-dramatisation. This becomes most apparent in the numerous self-portraits the painters of that movement have given us. Van Gogh and Gauguin were, of course, the first modern masters to take this deep interest in their own physical appearance, and it is known that they even exchanged self-portraits, Gauguin significantly inscribing his "les misérables". Among the Expressionists, there were painters

7

who recorded their own features almost every year, at least during certain periods of their lives. They showed themselves as heroes in the drama of life, isolated, with features that speak of bitter experiences and hands which underline that expression. The portraits they painted of other people were on the whole equally pessimistic and, like their own, often accompanied by features which indicated the sitter's character, occupation or attitude to life. Without going into detail, they thus told a whole story. Like the painters of the 19th century, they particularly liked to paint their friends, separately or in groups, but while in the past such works had been named "L'atelier" (Courbet) or "A studio in the Batignolles District" (Fantin-Latour), they now received such titles as "Exiles", or just "Friends" (Kokoschka). Even in portraiture it was not the external likeness that mattered, but once again the emotional significance and the mood which united these groups.

In the eyes of the Expressionist painters, man in all possible states had become a worthy subject of art: he was shown sick, drunk, in agony or in love; in his room, in city streets, or on the stage. It followed that he lost his individuality and became a type: the peasant, the clown, the frightened man, the corpse on the gallows. Frequently he was made to serve a purpose, for art could now be tendentious. The picture of a poor mother, of a prostitute, or of a dead man could be a violent accusation. At the time which led up to the First World War and the revolutions in Russia and Central Europe, many painters were inclined towards pacifism and socialism. They found it natural to disseminate their ideas through their works.

Others turned to religious subjects. But to them the figures of the Bible were utterly human. So they made them look humble and even uncouth, and their ecstasy or suffering so terrible that many were shocked by so much violence.

Not all Expressionist pictures, however, represent human subjects. There are landscapes — waving forests, heaving mountains and threaten-

8

ing seas — which seem to imply that the Expressionists' intercourse with nature was extraordinarily tempestuous. Even their still-lifes are full of a strangely dramatic animation as well as of symbolic meaning. They too are somehow humanised and express tension.

It is obvious that the Expressionists in no way shared the anti-literary attitude towards painting which has since become so fashionable. As soon as an artist emphasises the content of his picture, his art becomes automatically "literary". But only when it acquires the character of illustration, that is, when it slavishly accompanies the written word with pictorial elaborations, may we doubt its creative value. Expressionist art did not usually lean on literary invention, although it was sometimes inspired by certain writers. This inspiration varied between the adoption of another man's general outlook and the loan of names or types from his work. It is known that Dostoievsky much impressed some of the Expressionists, whose brooding figures might well have sprung from his novels. Even more direct was the influence of Strindberg, who was friendly with Edvard Munch, and whose pessimistic conception of the relationship between man and woman is reflected in the Norwegian painter's and also in Kokoschka's work; but both artists, Munch as well as Kokoschka, invented their own figures which were born from their personal experiences and their pictorial imagination, even if they dramatised them in the fashion of the Swedish author. The ties between writers and painters were often close ones, and the intellectual stimulation was mutual. Writers and artists fought a common fight for the liberation of art from academic and naturalistic conventions. No wonder that, after endless discussions of certain problems, they sometimes found themselves sharing the same subjects. Apart from this, there were many Expressionist artists who liked to express themselves occasionally in writing. Some of them produced essays on questions of art, others wrote memoirs, poetry and plays. This is true of nearly all the leading artists of the movement.

9

It would be wrong, however, to describe Expressionism as an intellectual movement. Like all artistic phenomena, it grew out of the mental climate of its period; but it was the outcome, first and foremost, of the desire of practising artists to renew their art. They based their experiments on the experience of other painters who had preceded them and learnt, like all true artists, much more from pictures than from theories. The predecessors to whom the Expressionists were particularly indebted were the Symbolists. We have already pointed out that Gauguin was responsible for some of the ideas which really bore their fruit when applied by the Expressionists, mainly the conception of painting as a means of communication between men and as an expression of thoughts or emotions; and of the importance of the human element. The French master had also introduced the subjective approach, a certain cult of ugliness, the symbolic colour and the principle of composition by flat undivided patches of paint.

But there were other artists who had helped to prepare the ground for the Expressionist movement. Van Gogh had used colour dramatically and painted landscapes which reflected his state of mind rather than the luxuriant nature of France. The Belgian James Ensor had given his strange imagination free play in his paintings of masks and skeletons which allowed him to accuse and mock a humanity from which he felt excluded: his self-portraits bear witness to the isolation to which he felt condemned, and they show this artist, who was twenty years older than most Expressionists, well on the way to self-dramatisation. Then there was Toulouse-Lautrec, devoted to the study of his models in true 19th-century fashion, but passionately interested in the human element, and in his satire surpassing the limits of objectivity. He not only taught following generations to look more compassionately at human faces, but added certain subjects — the stage, the circus, the prostitute — to the Expressionist repertory. But more important to the development of Expressionism was Edvard Munch. He was the isolated artist *par excellence*, as all his self-portraits prove; seated in front of the bottle, sick beside his bed, naked in hell, he saw himself as the hero of a continuous tragedy; and nature in his landscapes was an agitated and oppressive background to the fears and sufferings of man.

Munch, and even the older Van Gogh, are by some critics counted among the Expressionists, while in the eyes of others they belong to the predecessors. In fact art movements overlap, and it is a vain effort to separate and label them neatly. Expressionism proper is usually considered to have begun in the first years of this century in Germany, and more particularly with the foundation of the "Brücke" group in Dresden, in 1904, by some young painters the most important among whom were Kirchner, Heckel, Schmidt-Rottluff, Pechstein and Nolde. They lived in close community, studied the painted and graphic works of the early German masters as well as Negro art, which they were among the first to discover, made etchings, lithographs and woodcuts as well as large watercolours, and held their first exhibition in 1906. This group, which existed until 1913, may be said to have represented German Expressionism in its purest form.

More international was "Der blaue Reiter" (The Blue Horseman) group which came into being in Munich and counted the Russian Kandinsky, the Austrian Kubin, the Swiss Klee and the German Franz Marc among its members. These artists were almost from the beginning in touch with the members of the French *avant-garde*; Rouault, Braque, Picasso, and Delaunay exhibited with them in Munich, and their publication of 1912, from which "Der blaue Reiter" received its name, contained reproductions of the works of Rousseau, Cézanne, Matisse and many other French painters, as well as German, Russian and exotic primitive art. A reflection of all these elements can be found in the works of the "blaue Reiter" artists whose style was on the whole more decorative than that of the "Brücke", more lyrical, more open to the influences of Fauvists and Cubists and more inclined to renounce the representation of reality. Each one of these painters gradually took a different course. Klee gave up representation to achieve an unprecedented freedom of invention. Kandinsky became the first abstract artist. Both artists still had this in common: that they went along the road which led away from the objective reproduction of things seen, up to its very end.

It was in 1910 that Kandinsky wrote his first book, *Über das Geistige in der Kunst* (The spiritual in art), in which he explained the new conception of art as a spiritual manifestation. That year was one of the most memorable dates in the history of Expressionism. In 1910, too, "Die Brücke" held a great exhibition at Dresden. The painter Chagall came for the first time from Russia to Europe and, like the Douanier Rousseau who died in the same year, he delighted the artists of Paris by the strong element of naiveté and imagination in his works. Finally, one of the main figures of Expressionism, Kokoschka, left Vienna for Berlin, where he joined the newly founded art magazine "Der Sturm" (Tempest). This publication has long since been recognised as one of the most interesting documents of Expressionism, for it was a kind of melting-pot through which nearly everybody of any importance in modern art passed at some time or other. Its editor, Herwarth Walden, was fanatically devoted to the fight against realism and to all *avant-garde* movements. Very typically — and like many of his contemporaries — he hardly distinguished between Expressionism, Cubism, Futurism and abstract art; in fact, he was inclined to call them all Expressionism. What mattered to him was that works of art should be "the expression of a vision", or "the realisation of an emotion by the means of painting", and he attached great importance to the "autonomous life of the picture". Walden arranged exhibitions in various German cities as well as abroad, and it was due to his enterprise that thousands who lived far from the great artistic centres saw the works of artists who were then still highly controversial. Klee, Kandinsky,

Chagall, Delaunay, Picasso, Léger and many others had paintings shown in his galleries and were thus introduced to the public. The reception was often a stormy one. But Walden and his artists flourished in this battle of ideas, and it was at this time that many of the artists in question produced their best works. What interrupted the artistic life of that period was the World War which broke out in 1914. It dispersed the painters into every corner of Europe, and those who survived it came back with changed ideas.

Yet the end of Expressionism had not come. After the war, when revolutions shook the intellectual life of Russia and Germany, great museums opened their doors to the works of the new painters' most of whom were now well over thirty years of age. They became famous, obtained important teaching posts and saw their pictures reproduced as posters and postcards, while a great number of books was published to explain their art to the masses. Unfortunately all this came to an end when the Nazi régime took charge of the cultural life of Germany and Central Europe: after the works of the Expressionists and other moderns had been branded as decadent, they were condemned to oblivion, and only those who went into exile could continue to work. When the Second World War was over, they were remembered and brought back, to be once more exhibited and interpreted. But they now belong to history, for new generations of artists have taken their place.

This, at least, is what happened to the members of the actual movement of Expressionism. There were always artists outside Germany whose work bore all the characteristics of Expressionism, and who yet did not take part in the life of the movement. Rouault we have already mentioned. The Belgians had a movement of their own which they called "Flemish Expressionism". Soutine, who had come from Russia like Chagall, was certainly an Expressionist until the end of his life, during the last war. Even Picasso had Expressionist phases.

In America too Expressionism is a well-known phenomenon. It is, in fact, justifiable to speak of Expressionist tendencies which need not be connected with the movement itself. At times these may not be fashionable — just now, for instance, they are rather in the background. But they will probably always exist, as they have always existed in the past.

LIST OF ILLUSTRATIONS

Plate 1

Vincent van Gogh (born in Brabant in 1853, died at Auvers-sur-Oise in 1890)

THE SOWER

V. W. Van Gogh Collection, Laren

Born in a Dutch parsonage, Van Gogh began to work for a firm of art dealers at the age of 16. But having been attracted by Bible studies at an early age, he went in 1878 to live as a lay preacher among the miners of Belgium. Shortly afterwards he began to draw, using workers and peasants as his models. He also made attempts to paint in oils, using mainly dark shades of brown and grey. In 1886 he followed his brother Theo to Paris where he fell under the spell of Impressionist painting and Japanese prints; these taught him new ways of composition and lightened his palette. Two years later he moved to the South of France where Gauguin joined him at Arles. But after two months Van Gogh's restlessness culminated in an outbreak of mental illness which led him to attack his friend and then cut off his own ear. During the rest of his life, spells of lucidity and work alternated with periods of illness and internment at Arles and St. Rémy. In July 1890 he took his own life.

"The Sower" was painted at Arles in 1888. There are several versions, drawn and painted, of this subject which was inspired by Millet and had occupied Van Gogh for some time. The silhouettes of the tree and the man, which give the picture its rhythm and its depth, are reminiscent of Japanese woodcuts. But it is mainly the colour of this composition — the juxtaposition of purple, blue and yellow — which shows great boldness. Van Gogh often mentioned his love of yellow, which made him paint lemons, sunflowers, cornfields and, over and over again, the burning sun. It is the huge, golden disk of the sun, contrasted with the bare trunk of the tree which, in this canvas, seems to express through mere concentration of colour what the painter wrote in one of his letters: "A sun, a light which, for want of a better expression, I can only call yellow, the yellow of pale sulphur, pale lemon gold. How beautiful yellow is!"

Plate 2

Edvard Munch (born 1863 in Norway, died 1944)

THE CRY

Oslo Municipal Collection

Munch began his training at the School for Arts and Crafts in Oslo. In 1889 he held his first one-man show. His work was then that of a 19th-century realist. But in the same year he moved to Paris and there came under the influence of the Impressionists which was, however, soon supplanted by that of Gauguin and Symbolism. Munch's mental attitude to and conception of his art owed much to the intellectual movements of his day, and particularly to the Swedish writer Strindberg whose preoccupation with the problematic relations of the two sexes the Norwegian shared and reflected in his paintings. In 1892 Munch went to Berlin to show his work, which caused one of the great art scandals of the period. In 1894 he made his first prints. After years abroad he obtained, in 1909, a commission to paint murals for the university of Oslo. He spent the rest of his life in Norway where he worked in solitude. During the last twenty years he gradually abandoned the symbolic character of his art and adopted a new realism. His later work comprises portraits, groups of figures such as men at work or bathers, and landscapes. His prints — woodcuts, etchings and lithographs — were even more revolutionary than his paintings and made the greatest impression on the German Expressionists who learnt much from Munch's monumental compositions and psychological approach.

"The Cry" was painted in 1893. Years later Munch wrote a story entitled "Alpha and Omega"; it contains these lines which read like a description of "The Cry": "He ran along the sea. The sky and the water took on the colour of blood. He heard cries in the air and covered his ears. Earth, sky and sea trembled, and he felt a great fear." There is no need to know what the man in the picture is afraid of. He is a personification of fear, his whole body is bent by it, and his cry carries it across the landscape whose curves seem to pass it on and on. The anxiety which dominated Munch in those years expressed itself in every line. Only after he had suffered a break-down and recovered from it, in 1908, could his art assume a new stability. But then he was no longer an Expressionist.

Plate 3

Vincent van Gogh (born 1853, died 1890)

THE GOOD SAMARITAN

Rijksmuseum Kröller-Müller, Otterlo

A short time before his death, in May 1890, Vincent van Gogh wrote to his brother from St. Rémy: "I have also tried a copy of 'The Good Samaritan' by Delacroix." This was not the first time he had made a painting after the French master: a few months earlier he had copied one of his lithographs, a "Pietà", in oils. During the year he spent in the asylum of St. Rémy, Van Gogh liked to copy works by such artists as Millet, Daumier, and also Rembrandt, very often simply because he had great difficulty in finding human models — a problem about which he frequently complained to Theo — and used the figures which had been invented by his predecessors as a kind of substitute. He had proudly written about his "Pietà" that in spite of his illness he had mastered the difficult turnings and foreshortenings of the two bodies to perfection, and he could well say the same of "The Good Samaritan" in which the helplessness of the wounded man and the Samaritan's strength and care are admirably conveyed.

The scene takes place in a ravine of the kind Van Gogh had painted a few months before, and which he had also described in letters to the painter Emile Bernard and to his mother: rocky mountains on both sides, a small stream flowing towards the background, and a path following the course of the rivulet. The unhappy traveller's wooden chest lies opened on the ground, while two indifferent figures walk unmoved past the scene of the tragedy. The horse seems to tremble, and the grass is bent as though under a storm. Every outline, every brushstroke betrays the tension which filled the painter during these last months of his life. The subject of this work was particularly close to his heart, and through it he expressed all the compassion he had always felt for those who were poor and helpless. Van Gogh's "Good Samaritan" can hardly be called an Expressionist painting, but its subject-matter and the way in which this has been handled lead straight to the religious works of the Expressionists.

Plate 4

Georges Rouault (born 1871 in Paris)

DE PROFUNDIS

Musée National d'Art Moderne, Paris

Rouault is the only great contemporary painter who has devoted his art almost entirely to religious painting. He is a Catholic, and his spiritual world is that of J. K. Huysmans and Léon Bloy. His artistic career began in the studio of Gustave Moreau who taught him to paint in an academic fashion. But before that he had learnt to make stained glass windows, and his colours as well as the black lines which separate them still remind us of his familiarity with the stained glass of medieval churches. Under the influence of the Fauves he became a modern painter. His first original works, which date from the beginning of this century, belong to the field of social satire; they represent judges, prostitutes and clowns in a style new to French art, although Daumier and Toulouse-Lautrec had prepared the ground for these subjects. They were followed by the religious paintings for which Rouault is best known. Since then the long series of biblical figures, heads of Christ and crucifixions, has only occasionally been interrupted by profane subjects. Between the two wars the painter devoted almost ten years to the drawings which are an important part of his oeuvre. Like Rouault's oil paintings, these represent subjects which belong to social criticism as well as to religious art. It is obvious that certain ideas have haunted the artist all through his life, and that he has hardly ever found it worth while to look for subjects outside them.

The death scene which is represented in "De Profundis" could hardly have been chosen by any other living painter. Only a deeply religious man for whom life on this earth is but a preparation for eternity could have painted it. Many years ago, artists like Munch and Käte Kollwitz had chosen similar subjects, but theirs had been scenes of despair. In Rouault's painting, which was finished in 1946, it is the crucifix on the wall that dominates the whole composition. All other details in this canvas follow the lines of the cross, except the bent back of the kneeling woman which expresses sorrowful acceptance.

Plate 5

Emil Nolde (born 1867 in Northern Germany, died in 1956)

JOSEPH TELLING HIS DREAMS

Kunsthistorisches Museum, Vienna

Nolde, who was about twenty years older than most Expressionists, began his career as a painter in the Impressionist manner. After having studied at Karlsruhe and been employed as a teacher, he visited Paris, Berlin, Munich and Copenhagen. It was in Dresden, where he lived from 1905–1907 and, for a time, joined the "Brücke" group, that he became a modern painter. In 1909 he did his first religious pictures, using strong bright colours to build up his large figure compositions. Before the First World War he joined an expedition to the Pacific Ocean, and the natives he saw there and their art made a great impression on him, which is reflected in his work. Later he lived mostly in Berlin and in the country, in Northern Germany. He painted landscapes, still-lifes — pictures of masks and flower-pieces among them — often used watercolour, and also made many woodcuts. In 1937 over a thousand of his works were confiscated by the Nazi régime, but after the last war Nolde was again honoured as the grand old man of German painting. He has written the story of his life which was published in two volumes, in 1931 and 1934.

"Joseph telling his Dreams" was painted around 1910, when Nolde did several groups from the Old and New Testaments. Joseph is seen surrounded by his brothers who are jeering at him and plotting behind his back. He is smaller and more delicate than they are, his garment finer, his face proud and withdrawn. They are crude, barbaric, crowding around him like the terrible figures who mock Christ in Bosch's "Ecce Homo". The heads and hands have grown to a terrifying size, and there is no escape from their wild eyes and gestures. The green in their faces and the red colour of their thick lips underline their expression of hate. Nolde was convinced that the soul of man could be made the subject of painting, and the ancient stories of the Bible probably fascinated him because they illustrate the most elementary human passions. Without any regard for artistic or other conventions he recreated them, as they had never been before, in colours which did not correspond to any realistic notions, but which were able to express the excitement he himself felt and wanted to convey.

Plate 6

Anton Kolig (born 1886 in Moravia, died 1950)

DESIGN FOR A CURTAIN FOR THE SALZBURG FESTIVAL HALL

Wolfgang Gurlitt Museum, Linz

Kolig was a pupil of the Vienna Academy. In 1911 he showed the earliest of the large compositions which he has always preferred to paint. In 1912 he went to Paris; there he saw the works of the Fauves whose bold use of colour made a great impression on him. More important influences on his development were, however, the baroque frescoes with which the churches of his country had been decorated during the 17th and 18th centuries. The tradition of large, colourful and highly expressive figure compositions which had thus been established in Austria still had a hold over the young artists at the beginning of this century; they saw their ideal in such late baroque painters as Maulpertsch and Troger. Of all modern Austrian artists Kolig was the one who remained faithful to this ideal all through his life. His interest was always absorbed by the human figure, its movements and the technique of fresco painting.

When Salzburg built its festival theatre, Kolig was one of the artists called upon to decorate it with a mosaic and tapestries. After the last war a new festival hall had to be planned for which he was to design a curtain. One of his designs is reproduced in our plate. Representing a group of singing angels, it is painted in the same innocent spirit of worship and praise as similar groups by Botticelli or Van Eyck. Kolig's angels form a protective circle around a human figure who rises from the ground, holding a skull — a symbol of mortality — under his left arm; but his right hand points upwards, and the head is slightly bent as though listening to celestial sounds. This allegory, conceived in representational terms, is yet executed with the means of modern art: there is no descriptive detail, and the colour, arranged as in a joyful musical chord, is the carrier of meaning and emotion. Together with the dynamism of the composition — which baroque art and Expressionism have in common — the bold subjective colour characterises this painting as one that belongs at the same time to tradition and to our age.

Plate 7

Oskar Kokoschka (born 1886 in Austria)

PORTRAIT OF CARL MOLL

Österreichische Galerie, Vienna

Kokoschka studied at the Vienna School for Arts and Crafts and first exhibited in 1908. His earliest known paintings are portraits and a few still-lifes, done in a strangely unrealistic, almost hallucinatory manner, with delicate, almost morbid colours, a few graphic outlines and particular emphasis on eyes and hands. In 1909 he went to Switzerland, and it was there that he began to paint landscapes. Gradually his handling became freer, but also more nervous, until an impression of constant movement emanated from all his compositions. In 1910 Kokoschka moved to Berlin where he became a regular contributor to the magazine "Der Sturm", for which he made some of his most extraordinary drawings. After the outbreak of the Great War he joined the Austrian army, was wounded and in 1917 sent to a sanatorium near Dresden where he was able to continue his work. He now came under the influence of the German Expressionists whose most violent colour combinations he surpassed in his new figure compositions and landscapes. After the war he travelled in many European countries and the Near East, painting landscapes in a broadly impressionistic style and summing up every city as though it had a character. After 1931 he tried to settle to down, first in Vienna, then in Prague, but the advent of Nazism drove him into exile. During the last war he lived in England, trying his hand at political allegories, but always continuing to paint portraits and still-lifes as well. He now lives in Switzerland.

The portrait of Dr. Moll, who was a painter of Vienna and a supporter of the young Kokoschka, dates from the period immediately before the first war. Obviously a good likeness from the realistic point of view, it is also a typical example of Expressionist portraiture: the head is slightly elongated, in the manner of El Greco, the hands are emphasized, and the whole, from the grey hair down to every fold of the superbly modelled suit, vibrates with an inner excitement which betrays the painter's rather than the sitter's temperament.

Plate 8

Max Beckmann (born 1884 in Leipzig, died 1950)

SELF-PORTRAIT

Günther Franke Collection, Munich

Beckmann was always an outsider who had little in common with other artists of his time. After having studied at the Weimar Academy, he went to Paris where he made the acquaintance of Cézanne's work, which left its mark on his painting. Only after the war of 1914 and a long illness did he develop his own style in large figure compositions which showed that he was preoccupied with the problems of creating space in his canvases and that he had turned to certain medieval German masters for guidance. Biblical subjects like "Christ and the Adulteress" now alternated with scenes from modern life which had a nightmare quality, crowded as they were with strongly plastic figures, often mutilated and always mysteriously but frantically occupied. Gradually he achieved a greater simplicity of composition, his figures became more monumental, their modelling softer. Beckmann became professor of painting at the art school of Frankfurt in 1925, but had to resign seven years later because he was attacked by the Nazis. He went to Berlin and in 1937 to Amsterdam where he stayed all through the Second World War. His reputation abroad had meanwhile grown, particularly after he was awarded the first prize at the Golden Gate Exhibition of San Francisco in 1939. After the war he was appointed professor of painting at the University of St. Louis, but although he was very successful in America he finally returned to Germany. His work, often prophetic in its scenes of perversion and torture, culminated in a series of allegorical triptychs which show a new richness of form and colour, but which only reveal their symbolic meaning after thoughtful study of every detail.

Beckmann has done many self-portraits throughout his career. This picture probably dates from the period of 1934—1936 when he suddenly began to try his hand at modelling, as did so many contemporary painters — Picasso, Matisse, Chagall and Kokoschka among them. There is no unnecessary detail, only the concentrated face, the pale purple coat and the groping hands, and it is to this economy of means that the painting owes its forceful effect.

Plate 9

Max Beckmann (born 1884, died 1950)

VARIETY

Günther Franke Collection, Munich

Beckmann painted performing acrobats as early as 1923, when he completed a picture entitled "The Trapeze". Similar subjects occur again and again in his work; important among them were another "Acrobat on Trapeze" and the "Interior of a Circus Caravan" in 1940, and a great triptych called "The Actors" in 1941/42. This picture was probably also done during the first years of the last war. It shows a conjuror who produces fire from his mouth, a dancer who lifts one of her legs so high that it becomes the vertical continuation of the other, and behind her a woman horizontally placed in mid-air, undoubtedly ready to be sawn in half; musicians are seen in the background, and the heads of spectators along the lower edge of the canvas. What we see happening on the small, crowded stage is, of course, symbolic. As usual in this artist's paintings, there is a sinister element — the magician — which is confronted with the feminine, erotic principle. The relation between the two is not always clear, but here they seem to keep their balance. The dancer looks triumphant; but her turn is not the last on the programme, and what follows is bound to be more sensational and perverse than beautiful. This is how, in Beckmann's eyes, the actors on the stage of life behave. He, who explained that he had to live in cities because he loved people, was horrified and fascinated by their madness, cruelty and indifference, which he has represented in pictures of night life, torture scenes and mythological paintings. But apart from the subject matter, which he considered extremely important, there was always a second problem that preoccupied him: that of the pictorial space and the plasticity of his figures. "To transform three into two dimensions is for me an experience full of magic ..." He was an Expressionist by nature, but he had familiarized himself with the laws of Cubism. The result was a new kind of realism which gives his works their almost over-natural life.

Plate 10

Oskar Kokoschka (born 1886 in Austria)

STILL-LIFE WITH DEAD RAM, TORTOISE AND HYACINTH

Österreichische Galerie, Vienna

Kokoschka has painted still-lifes at all stages of his career. But only in his earliest days, and then again in more recent years, have they played an important part in his work. When he was quite young he tried his hand at them as at everything else, and they were done with the same seriousness, the same passion as his portraits and landscapes. Later large figure compositions and landscapes absorbed the painter almost entirely. Then, during the last war, when he was occupied with political subjects and concentrated on what he saw in his mind, but not with his eyes, he often turned to the painting of still-lifes as though to relax, as to something gay, colourful and — real. He painted watercolours of the flowers in his room, and occasionally of fruit or other things. Sometimes these still-lifes found their way into a corner of his large oil paintings, and there they became part of the story the picture had to tell. Kokoschka has never painted anything as graceful and as joyous as these flowerpieces: they are the expression of a serenity which he only acquired when quite mature. And they are, in this sense, a measure of the long way he has gone since his early years.

The "Still-life with Dead Ram" is the pictorial embodiment of the anxiety which oppressed the painter when he was young. Painted before 1910, it is like a late outcome of the decadence which had marked the arts around the turn of the century, a picture of death rather than of life — a real *nature morte*. The skinned carcass is surrounded by creatures which are alive, it is true, but they are all children of darkness and dampness: a tortoise, a mouse, a serpent and a salamander in an aquarium. One remembers those still-lifes of the 16th century in which the Old Masters painted their flowers accompanied by beetles, moths and other symbols of death, to remind us of the vanity of all earthly things. Even the white hyacinth is like an evil flower, reminiscent not of spring, but of decay.

Plate 11

Chaim Soutine (born 1894 near Minsk, died 1943 in Paris)

STILL-LIFE WITH HERRINGS

Katie Granoff Gallery, Paris

Coming from the art school of Vilna, Soutine reached Paris in 1913 and worked for a time at the École des Beaux-Arts. In 1916 he moved into the famous "La Ruche", a building where Laurens, Léger, Modigliani and Chagall had their studios. He passed through years of great hardship, but friends enabled him occasionally to spend short periods in the South of France where he liked to work. He painted still-lifes, portraits and landscapes, in a style that was vaguely influenced by his knowledge of El Greco, Goya and the German Expressionists, less by his French contemporaries. Obsessed by the colours which he applied with heavily loaded brushes, and highly subjective in his approach to models, he was one of the rare Expressionists in France. His temperament found release in the violent movement which seems to have passed over the surface of his canvases. His portraits, painfully distorted, come close to caricature, although there is hardly anything amusing about them. His passion for certain colours made him chose certain subjects: at one time he was fascinated by white, and so he painted pastry cooks and communicants; then again he was attracted by a strong red, and he painted pictures of bell-hops in a red livery. Soutine spent most of his life in Paris, working feverishly. At the time of the German occupation he left the capital and continued of paint in the French countryside; but he was overtaken by illness and had to be taken to a Paris hospital where he died a few days later. He was buried in the cemetery of Montparnasse.

The "Still-life with Herrings" was painted in 1916, the year Soutine became a citizen of "La Ruche". Nothing could be more tragic and more revealing than this picture of three dead herrings and two hungry, trembling forks on a black table. They suggest the life the painter led at the time, a grim and frugal struggle. Still-lifes, which had been the purest symbols of objectivity when Cézanne painted them, had once more acquired the capacity to express an attitude of mind — and in this case it happened to be a pessimistic mind.

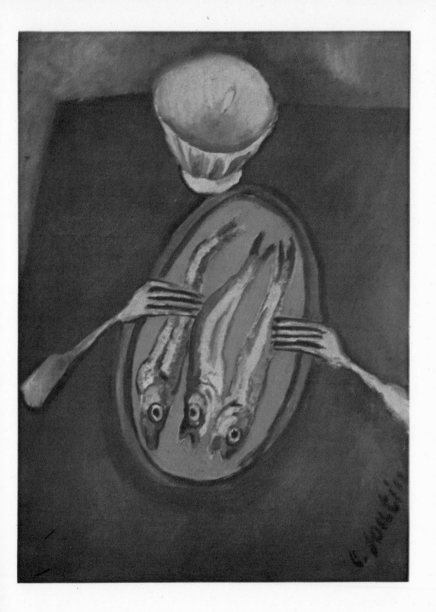

Plate 12

Georges Rouault (born 1871 in Paris)

POOR QUARTER

H. R. Hahnloser Collection, Berne

Paris has been painted innumerable times, particularly by the Impressionists, and in the more recent past by Utrillo, who continued to reproduce the picturesque corners of Montmartre as though the centuries had never touched the metropolis. It is true that the centre of Paris has changed little since the second Empire, while the ugliness and poverty of its growing suburbs naturally attracted few painters. That Rouault, who always went his own way, should have discovered them and felt the necessity to record their sordidness is not surprising, for he has always been moved by the misery in the life of modern man. The squalid activity in the streets where the poor grow up and move under an eternal burden is part of the same world which houses the terrible prostitutes, the hypocritical judges and melancholy clowns whom Rouault liked to paint. A profound pity for the men, women and children who are the inhabitants of the slums brought such pictures into existence. In the years 1929—1930 Rouault painted several related subjects: one represents a suburban funeral, another a factory at Gentilly, and there is also a set of six lithographs which the artist calls "Petite Banlieue". They all breath the same depressing atmosphere. The people in them, bent, pushing a pram or a coffin, are faceless; but the houses have eyes which express fear and pity; a shudder seems to run through the old buildings which grow higher and higher, forming an abominable sky-line. The whole is a piece of that hell on earth which man has made for himself. But even though this canvas is an expression of an innate pessimism, it is not an accusation like those heart-rending appeals that certain German Expressionists — particularly Käte Kollwitz — have produced. Rouault is satisfied with a statement of facts which speak for themselves, underlining them with his colour. And the painter in him, although inspired by his social conscience, has overcome the wretchedness of his subject and transformed the most unattractive matter into a work of art.

Plate 13

Max Beckmann (born 1884, died 1950)

RETURNING HOME

Günther Franke Collection, Munich

Painted in the middle of the war, in 1941, when the artist lived as a refugee in Holland, this picture is probably closely connected with something he had seen or that he could, indeed, see every day: a working–class or peasant family returning home after a day's work, all silently carrying their burdens and dragging their clogs across the ground, the children clinging to the mother's skirt. The light that seems to come from a source on the left throws black shadows on their path and makes the little procession look like a pathetic frieze that is drawn on a dark background; for it is night, and beyond the stage–like space that is thus lit up lies the unknown. Figures such as these have been painted before by Millet, Courbet, Van Gogh and Munch, who wanted to show that the working man can be represented in a work of art. But those in this canvas are not instruments of a social conviction, they seem to belong to a half-real world; they walk through the night as in a dream, and the sickle moon adds to the fantastic character of the scene. In their poetic isolation they are reminiscent of the Saltambiques of the young Picasso, who are equally oppressed by some unknown fear, a gloom they cannot shake off. At the same time one cannot help thinking of the real background that may have inspired such a picture: the hardships of occupation and the exile's nostalgia, both of which the artist knew. Beckmann has often invented compositions in which such experiences were not illustrated, but symbolized. "What I want to show in my work", he said, "is the idea which lies hidden behind so-called reality. I am seeking for the bridge which leads from the visible to the invisible . . . My aim is always to get hold of the magic of reality and to transfer this reality into painting — to make the invisible visible through reality. It may sound paradoxical, but it is, in fact, reality which forms the mystery of our existence . . My figures come and go, suggested by fortune or misfortune. I try to fix them divested of their apparently accidental quality . . ."

Plate 14

Georges Rouault (born 1871 in Paris)

HOMO HOMINI LUPUS

Musée National d'Art Moderne, Paris

"Homo homini lupus" was finished in 1944 and given by the painter to the National Museum of Modern Art. There can be no doubt about its meaning. It is one of the most violent accusations of man ever painted, and comparable only to certain scenes in Goya's "Disasters of War". Rouault's picture is a summing-up, not an actual report. Houses are burning, a man has been killed, and the sun is as red as blood. Goya wrote below one of his worst scenes: "This I have seen." Rouault, who is supposed to have said: "I don't believe what I see, but what I don't see", knew very well what happened during the war, and as though his painting could not make his thoughts clear enough, he wrote his terrible accusation in large letters underneath, comparing man with the most savage of animals.

Only an Expressionist would thus have used a picture to convey an idea: the choice of this particular subject alone would indeed have proved that Rouault was an Expressionist painter. The artistic means he employed are equally characteristic of that particular style: there is the simplicity of the composition, the monumental quality of the main figure which results from the suppression of all details, the symbolic red colour and the dark sky which is so impressively contrasted with the bright white of the shirt. Rouault, who has never actually taken part in the Expressionist movement, but whose artistic outlook and temperament happened to correspond with that of his contemporaries in Germany and other central European countries, shows in this moving work that the manner they had developed forty years before is still a possible and effective mode of pictorial expression.

Homo homini lupus

Plate 15

Vincent van Gogh (born 1853, died 1890)

CROWS FLYING ACROSS CORNFIELDS

V. W. van Gogh Collection, Laren

After a few weeks at Auvers-sur-Oise, Vincent van Gogh went to see his brother in Paris. This was his last visit, less than a month before his death. After his return to Auvers he wrote to Theo: "Once back here I have gone back to work — although the brush nearly slips from my hands — and, as I knew well what I wanted, I have painted three large canvases since then. They are immense stretches of corn under troubled skies and I have not been ashamed to try to express sadness, extreme solitude. You will soon see this, I hope, for I hope to bring them to Paris for you as soon as possible, because I think that these canvases will tell you better than I could do in words, what health and source of strength I see in the country."

No Expressionist painter has ever said more clearly what he meant by his landscapes: "to express sadness, extreme solitude." Yet Van Gogh had written on other occasions that cornfields to him, who had been brought up in the country, were symbolic of life, just as sowing meant creation of life, and cutting corn reminded him of death. The yellow colour in this picture still expresses the "health and source of strength" of which he also speaks. But it is a dark sky which hangs over the yellow corn, and the crows are, of course, bringers of evil. Hurried brush strokes which diverge in three directions indicate three paths across the corn, while others underline the high horizon and indicate the field's wavy surface. At the same time the tension of each stroke again bears witness to the painter's state of mind. A few days after completing this picture Van Gogh went out into a field and shot himself.

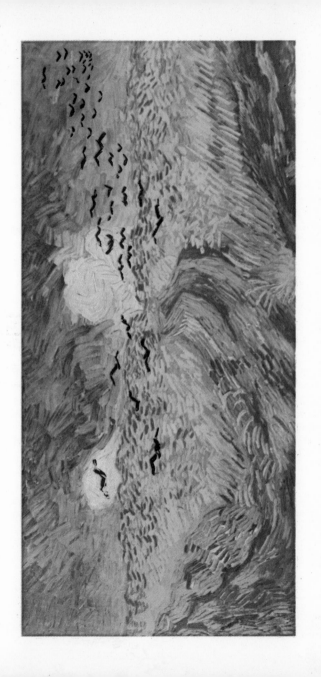

Plate 16

Vincent van Gogh (born 1853, died 1890)

ROAD WITH CYPRESSES

Rijksmuseum Kröller-Müller, Otterlo

After having left the South, Van Gogh wrote to Gauguin: "I have brought from down there a cypress with a star, a last attempt — a night sky with a moon without radiance, the slender crescent barely emerging from the opaque shadow cast by the earth — a star with exaggerated brilliance, if you like, a soft brilliance of rose and green in the ultramarine sky across which are hurrying some clouds. Below, a road bordered with tall yellow canes, behind these the blue *Basses Alpes*, an old inn with yellow lighted windows, and a very tall cypress, very upright, very sombre. On the road a yellow cart with a white horse in harness, and two late wayfarers. Very romantic, if you like, but Provence also I think." On another occasion he had written to Theo: "The cypresses are always occupying my thoughts, I would like to make something of them like the canvases of the sunflowers, because it astonishes me that they have not yet been done as I see them. The cypress is as beautiful in line and proportion as an Egyptian obelisk. And the green has a quality of such distinction." And in a letter to his friend Bernard, of June 1888, we find these sentences: "But when shall I paint the starred sky, that picture which preoccupies me. Alas, alas! It is really as that excellent fellow Cyprien says in J. K. Huysmans's 'En ménage': the most beautiful pictures are those one dreams while smoking a pipe in one's bed, but which one does not paint."

Strangely enough, none of Van Gogh's comments correspond with the impression we receive from the painting here shown, which is one of intense excitement, even of chaos — as though the earth and its trees had been set afire by the whirling stars. It almost seems as though the painter did not see that his cypresses looked like flames, and as though in this work, which was done two months before his suicide, his brush gave away a secret of which he was not himself aware.

Plate 17

Egon Schiele (born 1891 at Tulln, died 1918 in Vienna)

FOUR TREES

Österreichische Galerie, Vienna

Schiele, who studied painting at the Vienna Academy, exhibited for the first time when he was nineteen years old. As a pupil of Gustav Klimt, who was the best known representative of "Art Nouveau" in Austria, he had inherited a tendency towards linear composition which corresponded perfectly with his natural gifts, for Schiele was in the first place a brilliant draughtsman. His reputation as one of the most hopeful artists of the young generation was soon established, but his struggle to earn a living was nevertheless a very hard one. The portraits he painted were mostly those of friends, and even his drawings, which sold more easily, did not enable him to lead a carefree life. The outbreak of war in 1914 interrupted his career, which was thus cut very short, for he died, a victim of the European influenza epidemic, in 1918. Schiele has left mainly landscapes and portraits behind. Like Kokoschka, who was five years older and had begun his career under similar conditions, he had soon become dissatisfied with the decorative tendencies of "Art Nouveau" which were then prevalent in Vienna and had attempted to use his art to express something of the nervousness and tension he felt in the atmosphere around him. Schiele never reached the stage of technical experiment and distortion which is one of the characteristics of Expressionism, but his portraits are distinguished by a certain *morbidezza*, and his landscapes reflect a melancholy attitude reminiscent of the decadence of the *fin-de-siècle*.

The "Four Trees", which Schiele painted in the last year of his life, shows him as one of the artists who prepared the ground for Expressionism. Nature is still faithfully copied, but it is also interpreted in a manner which clearly reveals the painter's mood. Autumnal tints, bare branches and an evening sky are symbolic. Perhaps the shades of red and purple in the sky and the glowing sun speak of that gloom and desolation which lay over Europe at the end of the First World War.

Plate 18

Marc Chagall (born 1887 at Vitebsk, Russia)

I AND MY VILLAGE

Museum of Modern Art, New York

Chagall learnt to paint at the Imperial School for Fine Arts in St. Petersburg where he had arrived at the age of 18. Three years later he was on his way to Paris. There he lived in the same building as Modigliani and Soutine, became a friend of the poets Cendrars and Apollinaire and met the Cubist members of the École de Paris. Chagall himself painted nostalgic memories of his native country in a naive expressionistic manner, but soon these began to show Cubist influences. However, his subject-matter remained his own, and so did his approach to painting which was that of a man who tells dreams and fairy tales, or a poet who uses paints and brushes instead of pen and paper. In 1914 Chagall had his first one-man show, which was, characteristically, held in the "Sturm" galleries in Berlin. He was then on his way back to Russia where he spent the years of the First World War, took part in the revolution of 1917 and even became a Minister of Arts in his native city. But in 1922 he left again, first for Berlin, then for Paris which became his home in 1923. In the following years he painted, travelled, exhibited and illustrated many books, particularly the Bible, La Fontaine's Fables, Gogol's "Dead Souls" and his own memoirs. During the last war he found refuge in America, returning to France when it was over. His art, which had for a time reflected the tragic events in Europe, is now more lyrical than ever before.

"I and my Village" is one of the canvases Chagall painted in his first year in Paris. Like a dream, it is composed of apparently incoherent elements which have, however, a subjective connection: there is the face of a man who holds a flower, the head of a cow, a smaller cow that is being milked, a row of houses with a church, a peasant with a scythe, and a woman who stands on her head. Chagall, who had still painted fairly realistically when he came to Paris, had now learnt that, in order to make a picture, it was not necessary to follow the natural order of things too closely, and like a child he began to arrange his world in his own fashion, filling his canvas with his memories and the most beautiful colours he could find.

Plate 19

Marc Chagall (born 1887 at Vitebsk, Russia)

THE CATTLE DEALER

Kunstmuseum, Basle

Chagall tells in his memoirs that his grandfather was a butcher, and he says: "I have forgotten to remember you, little Uncle Neuch. I used to go out into the country with you to look for cattle. How happy I was when you consented to take me in your jolting cart." The connection between these memories and "The Cattle Dealer" is obvious. This was one of the pictures which delighted the artists of Paris because of its husophisticated approach to a world which was so far away that it seemed like a fairly tale. Chagall's block onuses and his cows at the trough, his high-booted peasants and village brides looked at first like figures from a picture book for children, until it was discovered that they represented that element of freshness, unself-consciousness and unspoilt imagination which had so long been found missing in western art. The very qualities which artists had been trying to find in the works of African peoples, in the art of the Middle Ages and in folklore, were contained in Chagall's pictures. No wonder that the poets of Paris dedicated poems to him and his reputation reached Germany where the artists of "Der blaue Reiter" and Herwarth Walden of "Der Sturm" were equally fascinated by his production.

Chagall was a born Expressionist, for to him painting was "a state of the soul". "The Cattle Dealer", which was painted in 1912, at first sight seems, it is true, relatively realistic, for nobody stands on his head, and all proportions are quite natural — although one soon notices that nearly all bodies are shown in profile, in the manner of some antique frieze, that the cart has only two wheels, and the mare carries an embryo foal visible in her inside. The colours are even more unrealistic. Like Franz Marc in Munich, Chagall painted red horses and blue cows because it suited his composition, and because he felt like it. He loved the colours he had seen in his home land: they are the gay, warm hues that can be found in all Slav decorative art, on costumes, cottages, crockery and icons. And the colours of nature would not have expressed what he wanted to say when he painted Russian village scenes in his Paris studio.

Plate 20

Marc Chagall (born 1887 at Vitebsk, Russia)

THE RECLINING POET

Tate Gallery, London

"The Reclining Poet" was painted in 1915, when Chagall had returned to Russia after four years in Paris. He had tried to settle down in his home town once more and had married Bella, "my fiancée in black gloves", as he had called his portrait of her in 1909. He now painted less from memory and absorbed fewer art theories than had been possible in Paris. As a result his pictures began to look different: they became more realistic and at the same time more lyrical. His outlines flowed more softly, and bunches of flowers made their appearance. He had left his cut-off figures and his contrasting colours behind in Paris.

But if he had found his home town again, he now suffered from a new nostalgia, for he was obviously an incurable romantic. "The Reclining Poet" is a typically romantic painting which tells the story of the town dweller who has come, pale and thin and elegantly dressed, to look for peace and solitude in nature. Chagall's young man is of the same family as Picasso's early harlequins, slender and melancholy, but Chagall may also have seen such figures among the members of the Russian ballet, which he frequented at the time of his first art studies at St. Petersburg. There is a fine expression of irony in the poet's folded hands and in his elongated proportions as well as in his smart shoes. This figure is contrasted in a telling fashion with the quietly grazing, robust animals in the background. The meadow, the trees and the farm house are depicted with a somewhat naive realism that the painter would have despised when still in Paris and surrounded by Europe's avant-garde. It shows Chagall in a new, pensive mood, still a poet, but less eccentric and less bold.

Plate 21

Robert Delaunay (born 1885 in Paris, died 1941 at Montpellier)

EIFFEL TOWER

Musée National d'Art Moderne, Paris

Delaunay was one of the links between the art of the Impressionists and Cézanne on the one hand, and the Expressionists on the other. He began as a "pointillist", but his dots were really small squares of contrasting colour. This manner, incidentally, is echoed in the paintings Kandinsky produced between 1905 and 1907. Delaunay soon arrived at a very personal version of Cubism which he applied to the representation of architecture. His first version of the Eiffel Tower, which he was to paint so many times during his career, dates from 1908/09. In 1911 he exhibited in the Salon des Indépendants and with the "Blaue Reiter" in Munich, and it was at about this date that he exerted a greater influence than any other French artist over such Expressionists as Marc, Feininger and Klee. In 1913 his work was seen again at the "Sturm" in Berlin. He had now begun to use colour for its own sake, as it were, or as the strongest element in his compositions, and it was this method that greatly impressed the German Expressionists, while it was the cause of his arguments with the Cubists of Paris: "I was the heretic among the Cubists. Great discussions with my friends who had banned colour from their palettes . . . I was accused of going back to Impressionism, of practising a decorative manner of painting, etc. etc." But this was not how he saw it himself: "I played with colours as one might express oneself in music by composing a fugue . . ." And this is precisely how Kandinsky and Klee, who also like to use musical analogies, came to use colour.

In 1915 Delaunay went to Spain and Portugal where he painted a series of still-lifes. In 1917 he worked for a time with Diaghilev. From 1921 onwards he lived mainly in Paris. He painted several portraits, those of the poets Breton and Aragon among them. After 1930 he painted a great number of purely abstract compositions in which flat discs of bright colour were a constant motif, but even in 1937 he still painted a picture of the Eiffel Tower, this time surrounded by revolving circles. Our version of the subject probably dates from 1926, when the painter had not yet ventured into abstract art. But here too "the colour alone is subject and form."

Plate 22

Henri Rousseau (born 1844 at Laval, died 1910 in Paris)

APOLLINAIRE'S MUSE

Private Collection, Paris

Rousseau's early life is not well documented, but it seems that he went to Mexico as an army musician in 1862, and he certainly took part in the Franco-Prussian war of 1870. After his return he was employed in a toll station on the outskirts of Paris, an occupation to which he owed his later epithet "le Douanier". It is likely that he had always painted and drawn, but it was not until 1880 that he signed his first pictures. Five years later he retired in order to devote himself entirely to painting. Apart from some advice which he had received from the academic artists he consulted he was self-taught, but his self-confidence was never shaken, although he had to pass through many hard years. When he first exhibited in the Salon des Indépendants his pictures were greeted with derision; but undeterred he continued to show landscapes, still-lifes, portraits and fantastic compositions until his unusual canvases attracted the attention of contemporary artists. In 1890 he made the acquaintance of Gauguin, Redon and Seurat, painters who were trying to overcome the exclusive influence of Impressionism by the introduction of new ways of composition, and who perhaps saw something in Rousseau's highly plastic paintings that corresponded to their own efforts. It was at about this time that he began to paint the exotic vegetation and animal life which some believe to be based on his Mexican memories, while others say that he found all his inspiration in the Jardin des Plantes. During the last decade of his life he found his place among the avant-garde of his day. Picasso, Delaunay and Kandinsky acquired his works. What they admired in them was the uninhibited directness with which Rousseau had expressed what he loved or what occupied him, and the instinctive rightness with which he transposed dreams and reality onto his canvas.

"Apollinaire's Muse" is one of those whole-figure portraits in a landscape in which his strangely contrasting qualities are combined: solidly built and finished with precision, it shows why Rousseau called himself a realist painter; yet an impression of magic emanates from the monumental black figure, and the trees and flowers belong to the realm of poetry.

Plate 23

TEMPTATION

Paul Klee Stiftung, Berne

Paul Klee (born 1879 near Berne, died 1940 in the Tessin)

Klee studied painting in Munich from 1898—1901 and, like most artists of the period, began his career as a follower of the 19th-century realists. His tendency towards the fantastic and his ironical outlook found their first expression in a series of grotesque etchings and in many drawings. His attempts to free his art from the fetters of realism were encouraged by several important encounters: in 1911 he met Kandinsky who was well on the way to abstract art; in 1912 he saw works by Delaunay and Chagall who were already using colour without reference to the natural colours of reality; he also went to Paris where he saw the works of the Fauves and the Cubists. More decisive still was a journey to Tunisia he undertook in 1913 and there he painted his first really colourful pictures. His earliest completely original compositions date from the war years. In these, real, invented and abstract elements are combined in a new manner: although there is no domain of life from which Klee does not draw inspiration — for plants, animals, human beings, landscapes and man-made objects serve him equally well — all realistic devices, such as perspective and natural proportions, have been abandoned. Art, no longer a reflection of the visible reality, has become autonomous. Klee at the same time felt the necessity to remain connected with a community and thus with reality, so he became a teacher at the famous "Bauhaus" where the arts and crafts were taught as two inseparable subjects. He belonged to its staff from 1921—1930. In 1933 he was forced to leave Germany. He died in Switzerland.

Klee once spoke of the line that "went for a walk". This is perhaps what happened in this picture: abstract lines walked up and down, always parallel, until they formed a shape, and when the shape was complete it had become a symbol. "Paths are established in the work of art for the eye of the spectator to follow." What he sees in the end is a winged form — an old symbol of virtue and holiness — being attacked by a snake or dragon. Klee has called this composition "Temptation". It was painted in 1934, a year in which he produced several pictures with religious connotations.

Plate 24

Paul Klee (born 1879 near Berne, died 1940 in the Tessin)

WITH THE EAGLE

Paul Klee Stiftung, Berne

"With the Eagle" was painted in 1918, at a time when Klee liked to paint pictures which have been described as landscapes, although they are, strictly speaking, compositions inspired by landscape motifs. There is a house, there are trees and a stag, but close to the alpine firs grow palm trees, and the farmhouse is overshadowed by the noble arches of original fairy palaces. The eagle seems to belong to the forest, but it is at the same time a heraldic bird, symmetrical and symbolic. Most mysterious of all is the eye in the centre: it looks at us, but we do not know who it belongs to. Flatly composed like a piece of tapestry, the picture yet seems to open up a secret depth, for the arches lead into an unlimited background that glows with colour. It gives a glimpse of a universe which owed its existence to Klee's imagination, his memories and dreams.

This is how his biographer, Clara Giedion-Welcker, describes this type of picture: "Elements of plant life and, most numerous of all, motifs of architectural provenance pass in dreamlike review as though emerging from the depth of memory; and frequently, hovering above, is an isolated eye, the painter's eye, the eye of the Creator — a feature which, recurring in just this solitary fashion, will become a familiar part of Klee's work. A transcendent poetic spirit seems to illuminate the physical world . . ."

Klee knew that an art as wholly unrealistic as his would not be easily understood. But to him it was a release, and he wanted others to enjoy it in a similar spirit; therefore he wrote in his "Creative Confession": "Come on, Man! Appreciate this holiday freedom which enables you for once to change your point of view as well as the air and let yourself be carried into a world which, by diverting you, will give you strength for the inevitable return into the greyness of the working day."